P9-DLZ-369

Queen
OF THE
Track

QUEEN
OF THE
TRACK

ALICE COACHMAN
OLYMPIC HIGH-JUMP CHAMPION

HEATHER LANG
ILLUSTRATED BY FLOYD COOPER

BOYDS MILLS PRESS
Honesdale, Pennsylvania

Acknowledgments

My deep gratitude goes to Karen Klockner, for guiding my vision and providing brilliant editorial insight; my first and last readers, Jamie Harper, Marty Lapointe-Malchik, and Mary Delaney, for their wisdom and support; my SCBWI Concord critique group, especially Helen Kampion, Sam Kane, Melissa Stewart, and Joannie Duris, for their excellent advice and feedback; and to Lee W. Formwalt, executive director, Albany Civil Rights Institute, Albany, Georgia, and Teresa Harris and Jan Brown for their valuable insights. Many, many thanks to the staff at the Alice Coachman Foundation, Olympic historians Stephanie Daniels and Anita Tedder, and Olympic silver medalist Dorothy Tyler for reviewing the manuscript and providing research assistance. A very special thanks to Floyd Cooper for bringing the story to life.

—HL

Text copyright © 2012 by Heather Lang
Illustrations copyright © 2012 by Floyd Cooper
All rights reserved
For information about permission to reproduce selections from this book,
please contact permissions@highlights.com.

Boyds Mills Press, Inc.
815 Church Street
Honesdale, Pennsylvania 18431
boydsmillspress.com
Printed in China

ISBN: 978-1-59078-850-9
Library of Congress Control Number: 2011939994
First edition

The text of this book is set in ITC Caxton Light.
The illustrations are done in pastel.

10 9 8 7 6 5 4 3 2 1

Photos credits: pg. 35, copyright © Associated Press, courtesy of Library of Congress
              pg. 36, copyright © Bettman/Corbis, courtesy of Library of Congress

To Jeffrey, Lucy, Jack, and Anna for inspiring me.
And to Dave for believing in me.

—HL

To the spirit of giving one's all toward excellence

—FC

ALICE COACHMAN WAS BORN TO RUN AND JUMP. On morning walks with her great-grandmother Rachel, Alice skipped ahead through the fields. She hopped on rocks. She vaulted over anything that got in her way.

As Alice got older, her papa told her to stop running and jumping. In the 1930s, running and jumping weren't considered ladylike. Besides, as one of ten children, Alice had lots of chores to do. She got up early to cook corn bread and eggs. After school, she washed the clothes and hung them to dry. She picked cotton and peaches with her older brothers and sisters and took care of the younger children.

Still, all Alice could think about was running and jumping. So when she was done with her chores, she'd sneak off to play sports with the boys. People said she was a "crazy fool," and she knew Papa would punish her. But she couldn't pass up a chance to run and jump.

In Albany, Georgia, like most of the South, black people didn't have the same rights as white people. Most white people wouldn't even shake hands with a black person. Blacks couldn't sit where they wanted on buses, and they weren't allowed in many public places. There were no gyms, parks, and tracks where Alice could practice running and jumping. She didn't let that stop her. She ran barefoot on dirt roads. She collected sticks and tied rags together to make her own high jumps. Alice jumped so high, she soared like a bird above the cotton fields.

When Alice was in seventh grade, the high-school track coach noticed her talent. He convinced her parents to let her go with the team to the famous Tuskegee Relays in Alabama. There she could compete against top black athletes from all over the country. For the first time in her life, Alice left Albany. She had never worn track shoes before or jumped over a real high-jump bar. Alice won first place anyway, beating high-school and college girls.

Alice didn't use her running talent only to win ribbons. One night in 1940, a tornado twisted into Albany, destroying homes and injuring many people. For two weeks Alice volunteered as a rescue worker. She moved so fast, she could deliver food while it was still hot. No one thought Alice was a crazy fool then.

That year, the track coaches from the Tuskegee Institute persuaded Alice's parents to let her finish high school at Tuskegee. The all-black school was known for its excellent high school and college, as well as its athletics. Tuskegee gave Alice a scholarship to cover her tuition. In exchange for her room and board, she cleaned the gymnasium and pool, rolled the clay tennis courts, and sewed uniforms.

Alice missed her family and worried about them a lot. Without any money, they had a hard time staying in touch. Sometimes the coach gave Alice stamps so she could write to them. One time she went home for a surprise visit, and her family had moved to a different house.

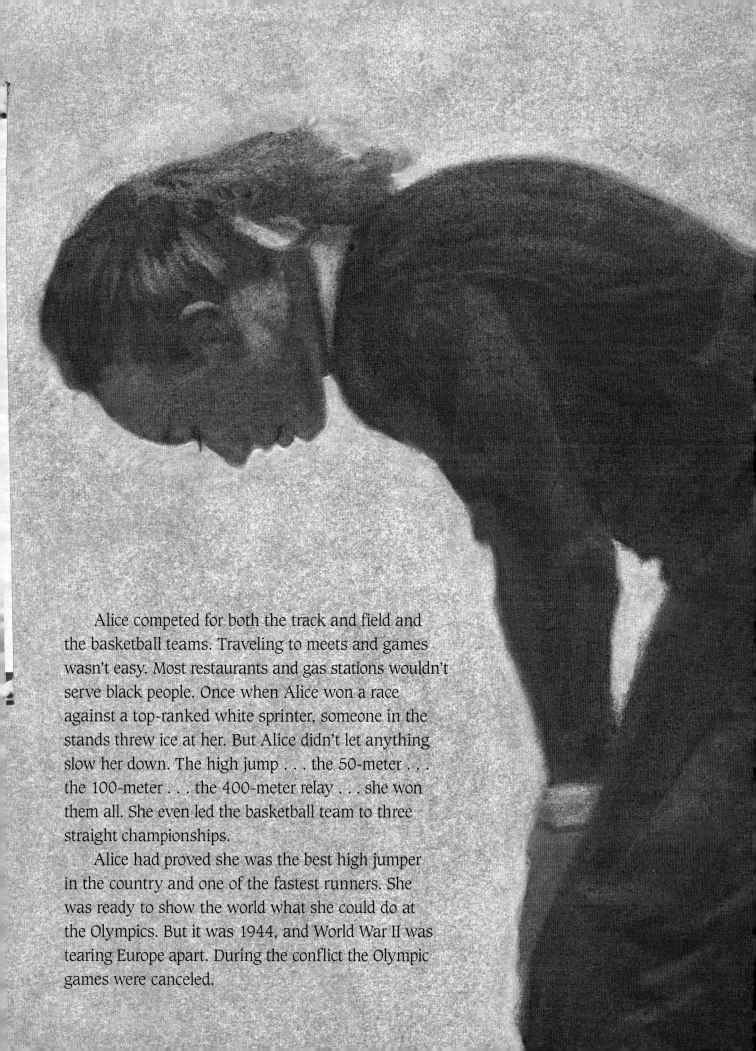

Alice competed for both the track and field and the basketball teams. Traveling to meets and games wasn't easy. Most restaurants and gas stations wouldn't serve black people. Once when Alice won a race against a top-ranked white sprinter, someone in the stands threw ice at her. But Alice didn't let anything slow her down. The high jump . . . the 50-meter . . . the 100-meter . . . the 400-meter relay . . . she won them all. She even led the basketball team to three straight championships.

Alice had proved she was the best high jumper in the country and one of the fastest runners. She was ready to show the world what she could do at the Olympics. But it was 1944, and World War II was tearing Europe apart. During the conflict the Olympic games were canceled.

When Alice was twenty-three, she graduated from the Tuskegee
Institute's junior college and went home to Albany, leaving the track
team behind. Alice trained alone, up and down the dirt roads:
Jogging
Sprinting
Jumping
Through the dust, she still kept sight of her Olympic dream.

When the war was over, Alice finally
had her chance. She qualified to high-jump
in the 1948 Olympics. Even though Alice had
never lost a high-jump competition before, she
wasn't sure she could win this one. The years
of hard training had weakened her back, and
jumping was painful. But this was the chance
she'd been working for all her life.

With her Olympic teammates, Alice boarded the SS *America* bound for England. On the seven-day voyage across the ocean, Alice met people from all over the world. One night the athletes were in charge of entertaining the passengers, so Alice performed a dance to "St. Louis Blues."

In London, Alice stayed with the other athletes on a college campus. They all lived together—black and white—joined by their dreams.

The war had taken its toll on the city. Bombing had left the streets littered with piles of rubble. Most people in England faced serious food shortages. Alice and the other athletes were often hungry and thirsty.

The cold English weather pricked her like pins, but Alice trained twice a day. And when she had time, she traveled around London and nearby towns, hopping from bus to bus. Alice could sit in any seat she wanted to admire the English countryside.

Despite the hardships that people faced in London, the Olympic opening ceremonies were spectacular. Alice marched with the other athletes into Wembley Stadium to the applause of eighty-five thousand spectators. The king of England proclaimed the Olympic games open, and thousands of pigeons took flight in the stadium. Alice had never seen so many birds soaring in the sky.

THE IMPORTANT THING IN THE OLYMPIC GAMES IS NOT WINNING BUT TAKING PART. THE ESSENTIAL THING IN LIFE IS NOT CONQUERING BUT FIGHTING WELL.

Alice waited eight days for her turn to compete. One by one her teammates lost their track events. With each loss, Alice became more determined. *Whoever beats me better set a record,* she thought.

Alice was America's last hope for a gold medal in women's track and field. Her toughest competition was Dorothy Tyler from Great Britain. Inch by inch they battled it out—5 feet 3²/₅ inches, 5 feet 4½ inches. The sand in the landing pit was thinning out and the landings were tough on Alice's back. 5 feet 5¹/₃ inches.

Even though it was getting late and all the other competitions were over, the king and queen of England and thousands of spectators stayed to watch.

At 5 feet 6⅛ inches, the bar was as tall as Alice. She'd never jumped that high in a competition before.

Alice focused on the jump.

She sprinted, pumping her arms.

She pushed off and flew . . . up . . . soaring . . . over the bar.

Her leap set a new Olympic record!

Dorothy jumped . . . and missed. But a jumper gets three tries to clear each height, and Dorothy cleared the bar on her second attempt.

The officials raised the bar to 5 feet 7 inches. Alice jumped and missed. Dorothy missed, too. After three attempts, neither athlete cleared the bar.

Alice wasn't sure what would happen next. There are no ties in the high jump at the Olympics. Then she saw her name on the board: "1 COACHMAN–UNITED STATES." Alice won because she had made the record-breaking jump on her first try.

On August 7, 1948, Alice Coachman from Albany, Georgia, became the first African American woman to win an Olympic gold medal. As thousands cheered, she stepped onto the podium. She had achieved her dream—a dream that started with a little girl running and jumping barefoot in the fields of Georgia.

The king of England presented her with the gold medal. "I'm very proud of you," he said. "Congratulations." Then King George VI shook Alice's hand.

More About
Alice Coachman

For most athletes, the greatest challenge is to master their sport. But for Alice Coachman, hurling herself over a 5-feet-6⅛-inch bar was far from her biggest obstacle. Born in 1922, Alice grew up very poor. She lived in Georgia, where black people were treated unfairly. Banned from public places, Southern black children weren't allowed to participate in most organized sports. To make matters worse, in the 1930s girls were expected to help with housework and be dainty. Alice's father punished her severely for sneaking off to run and jump. However, looking back, Alice believed that these enormous challenges gave her the determination and toughness she needed to become a successful Olympic athlete.

An exceptional runner and jumper, Alice earned nicknames such as "Queen of the Track," "Atomic Alice," "Track Ace," and the "Tuskegee Flash." She likely would have won several gold medals at the 1940 and 1944 Olympics, but both were canceled because of World War II.

After winning the gold medal, Alice returned to her hometown as a heroine. It was rare in Georgia to hold a celebration for a black person, but a special day was organized for her. A parade stretched for 175 miles. Yet segregation was still alive in the South. At her welcome-home ceremony, Alice was not invited to speak to the crowd. Whites sat on one side of the auditorium and blacks on the other. The mayor didn't even shake her hand. Still Alice felt support from many white people, who sent her anonymous gifts of congratulations through the mail.

Alice stopped competing after the 1948 Olympics but continued to accomplish great things. She went on to get her college degree from Albany State College. She became a community volunteer, a mother, a teacher, and a coach. She was the first black woman to endorse an international product when Coca-Cola featured her on its billboards. Named to eight halls of fame, Alice won ten straight U.S. national outdoor high-jump championships, a record that still stands today. In 1998, she was inducted as an honorary member of Alpha Kappa Alpha Sorority, the oldest Greek-lettered organization established by African American college-educated women.

Alice credits her success to the support she received from her family, teachers, coaches, and sometimes people she hardly knew. In an effort to give back and help others, she founded the Alice Coachman Track and Field Foundation, which supports young athletes and helps former Olympic athletes adjust to life after the games.

Many do not know Alice's story, since her gold medal came in the early days of broadcast television. But it was Alice Coachman who paved the way for future Olympic track stars such as Wilma Rudolph, Evelyn Ashford, and Jackie Joyner-Kersee.

"When the going gets tough and you feel like throwing your hands in the air, listen to that voice that tells you, 'Keep going. Hang in there.' Guts and determination will pull you through."
—*Alice Coachman*

Alice Coachman going over the bar in her record-breaking leap

More About the
1948 Olympics

At the 1948 summer Olympics, there was no Olympic Village. No new stadium. No extravagant entertainment. London was still in ruins from World War II. The streets were covered with bomb debris, and there were shortages of food, clothing, and gasoline. Many homes didn't have running water. Despite all these hardships, London managed to hold an unforgettable Olympics on a tiny budget and with less than two years to prepare.

London had to make do with what it had. The city transformed Wembley Stadium from a dog-racing track into the main sports stadium. An ice rink became the swimming pool. Athletes slept on camp beds in schools, military housing, and private homes. Many had to make their own uniforms and brought extra food from home. London buses transported athletes to where they needed to go. Countries pulled together to help out. Switzerland donated gymnastic equipment, and Finland sent the wood for the basketball floor.

Unlike today, in 1948 many Olympic athletes did not train full-time in their sport. They had other responsibilities. These athletes took time off from their full-time jobs to compete. Some had fought in the war. Some were mothers and teachers, and one was a concert pianist.

Recent Olympics—with their big budgets and years of preparation on the part of the host city—have been dramatically different from the 1948 games. But what the 1948 Olympics lacked in extravagance, it made up for in spirit, a spirit that grew from war, sacrifice, and hope.

Sources

Ashe, Arthur R., Jr. *A Hard Road to Glory: A History of the African American Athlete since 1946*. Vol. 3. New York: Amistad, 1988.

Blue, Molly. "Alice Coachman Jumped into History." *Columbus* [GA] *Ledger-Enquirer*, June 30, 1996, C1.

D'Avis, Richmondo. *A Journey to Gold: The Picture Story of Alice Coachman*. Akron, OH: Alice Coachman Track and Field Foundation, 1996.

Hampton, Janie. *The Austerity Olympics: When the Games Came to London in 1948*. London: Aurum Press, 2008.

Rhoden, William C. "Good Things Happening for One Who Decided to Wait." *New York Times*, April 27, 1995.

Roberts, Carolanne Griffith. "Southerners: Making a Difference." *Southern Living*, September 1, 2000.

Roulhac, Nellie Gordon. *Jumping over the Moon: A Biography of Alice Coachman Davis*. Philadelphia: privately printed, 1993.

Schefter, Adam. "Know Her from Adam: Alice Coachman." *Denver Post*, June 27, 2004, B-04.

Tricard, Louise Mead. *American Women's Track and Field: A History, 1895 through 1980*. Jefferson, NC: McFarland, 1996.

Weiner, Jay. "A Place in History, Not Just a Footnote." *Minneapolis Star Tribune*, July 29, 1996.

Video

National Visionary Leadership Project. "Alice Coachman." Online video interview.
visionaryproject.org/coachmanalice

YouTube. "1948 London Olympics High Jump (Amateur Footage)." Posted February
1, 2008. Online video clip. youtube.com/watch?v=Xzdu4GI_ZHI

Websites

All websites active at time of publication

Alice Coachman Foundation. alicecoachman.org
SR/Olympic Sports. "Alice Coachman."
www.sports-reference.com/olympics/athletes/co/alice-coachman-1.html
Official Report of the Organising Committee for the XIV Olympiad.
la84foundation.org/6oic/OfficialReports/1948/OR1948.pdf

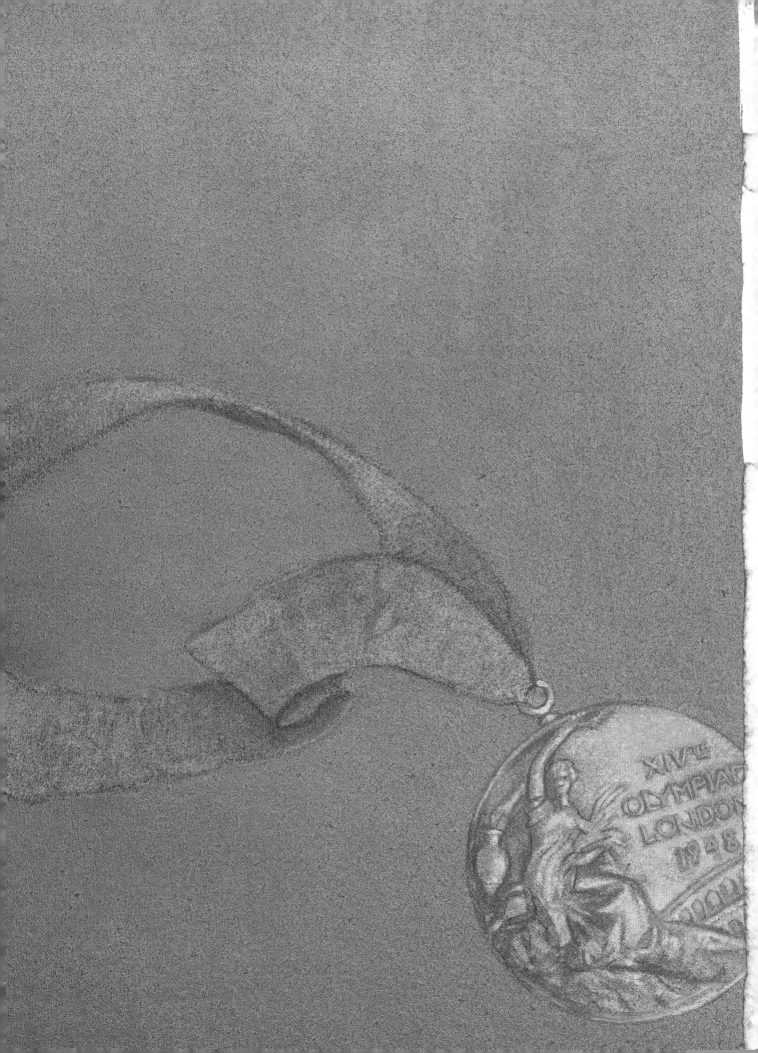